See What I Can Do!

An Introduction to Differences.

Jon Roberts

Illustrations Hannah Rounding

My daughter is autistic and has ADHD. Her friends in school often ask why she does the things she does, such as wave her hands, or why she doesn't talk. Children are very inquisitive and want to understand why other people live and act in different ways. They want to learn about diversity.

After speaking to friends and family, we decided to write this book to help raise awareness in school and at home and to share real-life stories direct from children around the world who live with disability.

Jon Roberts

See What I Can Do!
Published in Great Britain in 2021 by Graffeg Limited

Written by Jon Roberts copyright © 2021. Illustrated by Hannah Rounding copyright © 2021. Designed and produced by Graffeg Limited copyright © 2021.

Graffeg Limited, 24 Stradey Park Business Centre, Mwrwg Road, Llangennech, Llanelli, Carmarthenshire, SA14 8YP, Wales, UK. Tel: 01554 824000. www.graffeg.com.

Jon Roberts is hereby identified as the author of this work in accordance with section 77 of the Copyrights, Designs and Patents Act 1988.

A CIP Catalogue record for this book is available from the British Library.

ISBN 9781913733896

1 2 3 4 5 6 7 8 9

MIX
Paper from responsible sources
FSC
www.fsc.org
FSC® C014138

See What I Can Do!

An Introduction to Differences.

Every child is different. Some are loud,
they love talking and showing off.
Others are quiet and like to be on their own.
Some have differences that you can see, while others
have differences that may not be so obvious.
We are all unique. We all have our own lives, our own dreams,
and our own talents. Let's see what we can do.

GRAFFEG

4

Music and dance

Molly and Jillian are walking to school with their friends. They are talking about the things they enjoy.

"I love playing music," Molly says, pointing to her cello.

One of the other girls points to Molly's hands. They look a little different from other children's. "But, how can you play?" the girl asks.

Molly smiles. "I might look different, but that doesn't mean I can't do things. I just have my own special way of doing them."

Jillian nods. "That's like me with dance. My legs are different lengths, and I have to wear a special shoe to help me walk properly. But that doesn't stop me from competing. I have won lots of awards for my dancing."

"Wow!" says her friend. "I never knew you could do so much!"

Molly grins. "When I'm older I want to be a teacher so I can help teach children about limb differences. I want everyone to know that being different doesn't mean you can't do anything you want!"

There are so many ways to talk

Isabella, Axel and Christopher are building with blocks. Axel stacks his blocks as high as a tower. One falls to the ground and makes a loud bang, but Axel doesn't notice.

"I don't like loud sounds and bright lights," Axel explains. "They scare me, and make it hard for me to concentrate. That's why I wear headphones. They help block out the noise."

Isabella nods. "I love being around people, but I find it difficult to talk with them." As she speaks, Isabella moves her hands. She uses Makaton, a form of sign language. "I try my best to talk, but sometimes my words don't come out right. That's why I use my signs. They help to make sure I'm understood! But I do want to communicate better. I like to practise words when I'm on my own at home. I hope one day they'll be as clear as my signs!"

Nearby, Christopher builds a rocket ship. He pretends to be an astronaut. Christopher doesn't talk with words at all. He uses pictures and cards when he wants to say something.

Isabella, Axel and Christopher are autistic. You can't always tell if someone is autistic.

Many autistic people find it difficult to communicate with people and connect with the world around them. But they keep trying, every day!

(Say: AW-tiz-um)

Words can be tricky

Bradly and Hunter love playing football.

"OK everyone, get in from-from-fromation," Bradly calls to his friends. He tries to smile, but he knows he didn't say the word correctly.

"Do you mean formation?" one of his friends asks.

Bradly nods. "I have dyslexia," Bradly explains. "That means I have trouble with numbers and letters. My brain flips them around. It feels a bit like a brain scramble."

"Same here," says Hunter. "When I'm reading a book, the letters all dance around the page. If I have to read aloud, I take a deep breath before I start. I take my time when I'm reading and, when I finish, I smile."

"Dyslexia?" Bradly's friend is a bit confused. "Isn't that just about reading letters?"

Bradly shakes his head. "Most people think that, but dyslexia is more than just reading. I struggle with saying big words. And I have difficulty spelling and writing."

"Sometimes, I find it really hard finding the right words to say," Hunter adds.

"Me too, but I'm working on it!" says Bradly, proudly. "I have a strong imagination, and I love coming up with new stories and ideas even if expressing them is hard. When I'm older I want to be a film director. Then everyone will get to hear what I have to say!"

(Say: dis-LEK-see-uh)

Someone else's glasses

Anna and Caitlin are playing dolls with their friends.

"Uh-oh, Anna," her friend says. "Your doll's hair is getting knotted!"

"I sometimes struggle with brushing dolly's hair – and my own," Anna says. "Dressing myself is hard, too. Sometimes I put my clothing on backwards, and I'm always bumping into things."

Caitlin smiles. "I do that, too. I can trip over thin air."

"Isn't that normal?" their friend asks. "I trip sometimes, too."

Caitlin shakes her head. "We have dyspraxia. That means our brains make things like writing, running, and balancing hard to do."

"Having dyspraxia is like using the wrong hand to do things while wearing someone else's glasses," says Anna. Caitlin giggles at the thought of Anna wearing her granny's glasses!

"Huh," their friend says. "So things that are easy for me may be hard for you?"

"Exactly," Anna says. "Like painting. I love art, but I tend to get more paint on me than on the paper!"

"I like to talk to myself and think about what I'm going to say or do next," Caitlin says. "Some people may think it looks funny, but I don't care. It helps me get things right."

Caitlin and Anna's friend smiles. "Well, if you ask me, it's not weird. It means you have your own style. And that's cool!"

(Say: dis-PRAK-see-uh)

How many stripes on a zebra?

Josie and Piper are drawing animal patterns on a huge piece of paper.

"I love school," says Josie. "Especially art. I really like drawing shapes and patterns in loads of different colours. And I'm excellent at English. I always get high grades for my stories. But maths? Ugh! The numbers are so confusing. They seem to float around in my head and my brain is always changing them into other numbers."

Piper nods. "Having dyscalculia can be hard. It makes it tricky to learn or understand numbers. It's really great that the other kids in our class try and help us. The songs they sing and the stories they make up about numbers help me to remember my times tables."

"I wish other people understood that dyscalculia isn't something that will go away," Josie says. "I'll always have it, but I am still just as smart as them."

Piper looks at their drawing. "Smart, and talented. Look how beautiful our animal patterns are!"

(Say: duhs-kal-KOO-lee-uh)

Paying too much attention

Jaden and Elsie love performing.

"I have a *lot* of energy," says Jayden. "I absolutely love telling funny and colourful stories. But sometimes all that energy gets me in trouble, particularly in school. I find it difficult to sit still and concentrate on my schoolwork, and I talk all the time."

Elsie nods. "A lot of people think I can't pay attention or sit still for very long. They think I'm being naughty and trying to cause trouble, but I'm not. The problem is, I pay too much attention! I see every detail, hear every sound, and pay attention to them all at once. With so much in my brain, I sometimes forget what I'm doing, or I pay attention to the wrong things."

Jaden and Elsie have attention deficit hyperactivity disorder – or ADHD for short. Someone with ADHD might find it hard concentrating and controlling their body, so might move around a lot.

"It's tough," says Jayden. "Sometimes, I feel like Sonic the Hedgehog, always running at top speed and never stopping to do one thing."

"I know what you mean," says Elise. "Some days I wish I could slow down and act like a turtle."

Giggling, the girls get on all fours. "Who says we can't be turtles?" Jayden says. "Last one to the wall wins!"

(Say: A-D-H-D)

That little bit extra

Sadie, Summer and Lee are in the hall. They are pretending to be ballet dancers.

"I'm smaller than my friends," says Sadie. "But I'm super strong. And I love gymnastics."

"I love dancing and singing," says Summer. "It can be hard for me to do all the moves because my muscles are still getting stronger, but I know one day I'll be a really great dancer!"

Lee laughs. "My friends think I'm pretty cool, because I have a superpower. I can make even the grumpiest people smile, and my hugs are THE BEST!"

Sadie, Summer and Lee have Down's syndrome. That means their chromosomes are different. Chromosomes are the body's building blocks. Everyone has them, but people with Down's syndrome have an extra one. That makes their bodies develop differently.

Lee adds, "Mum says having an extra chromosome makes me who I am. She says it makes me special. And even better, she says it gives her more of me to love!"

(Say: Down SIN-drowm)

Lots of snot!

Ashley is browsing the Internet on her school computer. She is showing her friend a website on cystic fibrosis. Cystic fibrosis is a disease that affects Ashley's lungs and makes it hard for her to digest food.

"I love doing all the things my friends love to do," Ashley says, "but I struggle with breathing and breaking down mucus. That means snot."

"Eww," says Ashley's friend. "Snot?"

Ashley nods. "I get sick very easily, which means lots of snot! For me to stay healthy, it's important for my friends to wash their hands so they don't spread germs to me."

Ashley's friend smiles. "I'm glad to know that. What else can you do to stay healthy?"

"Well, my body has difficulty breaking down nutrients from food, so I have to make sure I eat the right things. That means I have to eat a lot of fatty foods like nuts and cheese," says Ashley. "But hey, it could be worse. After all, who doesn't like cheese?"

(Say: SIS-tik fi-BROH-sis)

Super-fast and flying

Bryson is in the lunchroom. His teacher, Miss Black, is helping him eat his cheese sandwich.

Bryson has muscular dystrophy. Even though he looks like everyone else, his body is different. "I'm not as strong as other boys my age," Bryson says between mouthfuls. "That's because my muscles keep getting weaker, instead of getting stronger. I get tired a lot too. And my muscular dystrophy affects my balance. I used to love riding my bike, but I had to stop because I kept falling off."

"That must be hard," says Miss Black.

"It is. I just want to be like my friends, but when you have muscular dystrophy, it slows you down. I use a wheelchair, and I'm learning to go super-fast, but I can't always do what my friends do. I never give up trying, though! And there's one thing I can do no matter what: travel! I love travelling with my parents to different places around the world, meeting new people, and learning their cultures and what they understand about muscular dystrophy."

(Say: MUH-skyoo-ler DISS-truh-fee)

Movement and song

Thandie and Nora are in the park, singing.

"I like singing," says Thandie, "but what I really love is swimming. If I could, I would live in the big blue sea. I would play with dolphins and sea turtles and collect seashells."

"Well, I love walking," says Nora, "but I struggle with steps, pavements, and stairs. Using my hands is hard, too. Holding a pencil or a spoon is tough. So is tying my shoes! I don't let it get me down, though. And I'm doing physical exercises to get stronger."

"Me too!" says Thandie. "I have trouble sitting up and moving around on my own, so I use a wheelchair to help me. I need to do regular exercises so that my muscles can become strong and I can learn to move my body better."

Thandie and Nora have cerebral palsy.

"For most people, their brains tell their body what to do and when to do it," says Nora. "But cerebral palsy jumbles those messages and it makes it hard for me to walk, talk, or eat."

"If someone sees me sitting on my own, I always hope they will say hi and ask me to play," Thandie says.

Nora smiles and nods. It's nice to have a friend who understands.

(Say: SER-ee-brul PAWL-sy)

Hearing with your eyes

The school bell rings, and the children go into the gym to play basketball.

MaryAnn, Anthony and Louis walk at the front of the line. That way they can look back and see people talking. All three have hearing loss. That means they have difficulty hearing the world around them.

"When I was very young, I used a hearing aid," said MaryAnn. "I learned to talk, too. Now I am totally deaf, so I use sign language. I make shapes with my hands to talk to other people."

Anthony touches his hearing aid. "Sometimes, my friends talk too fast. They get mad when I ask them to repeat themselves. I wish they would talk clearly and slowly and not scream at me."

Louis nods. "When I first started school, I had a hard time. People thought I was being rude, and not paying attention. Then the doctor realised I was deaf in one ear. I've learned that if you speak clearly and face me, I can read your lips."

"I'm glad we are able to walk at the front of the line," says MaryAnn. "That way we can see people's lips. When people don't talk in front of me, I get very sad. I cannot join in the fun. It makes me happy when we play together and I can understand what people are saying."

Sight and sound

Mina is in the music room, playing a piano.

"I love coming to school. Music is my favourite lesson," she tells her friends. "I'm particularly good at playing the piano and wind instruments. I have low vision, which means I can't see very well. But my ears work just fine! That's why I like music. I love listening to all the beautiful sounds the instruments make."

"I am learning to read large print," says Adeela. "I use a magnifier, which helps make the words bigger. My computer in school is great. It has a text reader that reads the words out loud so I can hear them."

"I can't see as much as other kids, but with a little help I can do anything I want," says Mina. "I love climbing trees, playing sport, reading about unicorns, chasing my brother, and—"

"Drawing rainbows!" Adeela interrupts with a giggle. "I have some sight left, and I'm getting the most out of it!"

Enjoy what you love

Chloe, Cami and Indie are in the playground. All around them the other kids run and jump. But the three girls can't join in with them, as they all have spina bifida. This means there is a gap in their spine.

Indie says, "I don't like anyone pushing my wheelchair, unless I am super tired. But I do like to go as fast as I can all by myself!"

Chloe agrees. "Me too. Zooming down the hall is so much fun! But I love dancing and music even more. I can't walk, so I dance sitting on the floor."

Cami has a frame to help her walk. "I struggle with running and climbing things. I know my brain is sending the right messages, but they keep getting lost on their way to my legs! But that's okay. There are lots of things I can do without my legs. I love writing stories, camping with my friends, and making things."

"Spina bifida never stops me from what I love doing," says Indie.

"If I could tell other children with spina bifida one thing, it would be to always keep doing what you love," says Chloe. "You have this amazing story. Share it and help others!"

(Say: SPY-na BIFF-ee-dah)

When things just stop

Lucas, Poppy and Leah are sitting in the shade, playing card games.

"Lucas, it's your turn," says Poppy. "Lucas? Are you listening?"

Lucas smiles. "Sorry, I was looking at the trees. I hope I didn't scare you. Sometimes, when it looks like I'm daydreaming, I'm really having a seizure. That means my brain freezes if it gets too busy. That happens to me because I have epilepsy."

"When I have a seizure, I stand up in class and walk around clapping my hands," Leah says. "My seizures are called focal seizures. I don't always know what I'm doing when I have a seizure, but I do know I'm always tired afterwards and need to rest."

"I have tonic-clonic seizures," Poppy says. "They make my body shake all over and I often stop breathing. The name sounds a bit funny but it can be pretty scary. Luckily, I have Fin, my supercool service dog. He goes everywhere with me. The problem is, people think he's a pet. I wish that people knew that you aren't supposed to pet service dogs when they're working. When you pet them, they stop helping their owner. That's when a seizure could happen, and I could be in real trouble!"

Leah says, "When I grow up, I want to train service dogs just like Fin."

(Say: EH-puh-lep-see)

Splashing around

Olivia, Xavier and their friends are learning to swim.

"I love swimming and playing outside," says Olivia. "But I get tired very easily and have to rest. If I get too tired, I could bump into something."

"I bump into things all the time," Olivia's friend says. "It's not that big a deal."

"It is for me," Olivia explains. "My bones are super fragile. If I bump into something, they could break! Once, I got a cold and coughed so hard, I broke a rib!"

"Wow!" Olivia's friend says. "I never knew that!"

Xavier nods. "Olivia and I have brittle bone disease. That means our bones can break really easily. It's so hard. I'm smaller than my friends and I have rods in my legs to support my bones."

"I have to be really careful," says Olivia. "That's why I have Betty, my service dog. She picks things up if I drop something accidentally. She's always there if I get upset or if I start to worry about hurting myself."

Xavier grins. "Having brittle bones is tough, but it doesn't stop us from having fun!" Kicking up some water, he splashes his friends. "See!"

My cool inhaler

The school bell rings to signal the end of the day. The children stream out of their classrooms and start making their way home.

Ella and Jake walk home together, kicking a tin can to each other and laughing.

Jake loves running around and having fun with friends. "When I run around a lot, I sometimes find it hard to breathe. I have to use my inhaler to make it easier."

"Tell me about it!" says Ella. "Sometimes, it feels like I have an elephant sitting on my chest. It squeezes all the air out of my lungs, and I can't fill them back up."

Ella and Jake have asthma. This means that sometimes they find it difficult to breathe and sometimes wheeze and cough a lot. They have to be careful when they catch a cold, when there's lots of pollen or dust in the air, or if the weather is very cold.

Being different can be a challenge for many children, but that won't stop them from loving every minute of life!

(Say: Az-muh)

Useful terms and links

ADHD (Jaden and Elsie, p.14)
A condition affecting a person's behaviour. They may have difficulty concentrating or keeping still. For information, advice and support visit www.adhdfoundation.org.uk.

Asthma (Ella and Jake, p.35)
A common lung condition that causes occasional breathing difficulties. For information, advice and support visit www.asthma.org.uk.

Autism (Isabella, Axel and Christopher, p.6)
A spectrum condition that affects people in different ways. Like all people, autistic people have their own strengths and weaknesses.
For information, advice and support visit www.autism.org.uk.

Brittle bones (Olivia and Xavier, p.32)
A genetic disorder characterised by fragile bones that break easily.
For information, advice and support visit brittlebone.org.

Cerebral palsy (Thandie and Nora, p.22)
A lifelong condition that affects a person's movement and co-ordination.
For information, advice and support visit www.cerebralpalsy.org.uk.

Cystic fibrosis (Ashley, p.18)
An inherited condition that causes sticky mucus to build up in the lungs and digestive system. This can result in lung infections and problems digesting food.
For information, advice and support visit www.cysticfibrosis.org.uk.

Deafness and hearing loss
(MaryAnn, Anthony and Louis, p.25)
This can be both temporary or permanent and can affect all ages. For information, advice and support visit bda.org.uk.

Down's syndrome (Sadie, Summer and Lee, p.17)
This occurs when someone is born with an extra chromosome. For information, advice and support visit www.downs-syndrome.org.uk.

Dyscalculia (Josie and Piper, p.13)
A difficulty understanding numbers which can lead to a range of problems with mathematics. For information, advice and support visit www.dyscalculiaassociation.uk.

Dyslexia (Bradly and Hunter, p.9)
A common learning difficulty that can cause problems with reading, writing and spelling. For information, advice and support visit www.bdadyslexia.org.uk.

Dyspraxia (Anna and Caitlin, p.10)
A neurological condition which affects muscle co-ordination and perception. For information, advice and support visit www.dyspraxiauk.com.

Epilepsy (Lucas, Poppy and Leah, p.30)
A condition that affects the brain and causes frequent seizures. Seizures are bursts of electrical activity in the brain that temporarily affect how it works. They can cause a wide range of symptoms.
For information, advice and support visit www.epilepsy.org.uk.

Muscular dystrophy (Bryson, p.21)
A gradual weakening of muscles, leading to increasing difficulty with mobility and bodily functions. For information, advice and support visit www.musculardystrophyuk.org.

Spina bifida (Chloe, Cami and Indie, p.29)
This occurs when a baby's spine and spinal cord does not develop properly in the womb, causing a gap in the spine.
For information, advice and support visit www.shinecharity.org.uk.

Visual impairment (Mina and Adeela, p.26)
There are different types of eye conditions or diseases that can lead to sight loss, such as glaucoma and cataracts. Complete blindness happens in few people - many affected by sight loss still retain some vision. For information, advice and support visit www.rnib.org.uk.

General

Mencap
www.mencap.org.uk/learningdisability-explained

Learning Disability Today
www.learningdisabilitytoday.co.uk

Rare Disease UK
www.raredisease.org.uk

Scope
www.scope.org.uk

Disability Rights UK
www.disabilityrightsuk.org

My AFK
www.my-afk.org